Exculpatory
Lilies

BOOKS BY SUSAN MUSGRAVE

POETRY

Origami Dove
When the World Is Not Our Home: Selected Poems 1985-2000
The Obituary of Light: Sangan River Meditations
What the Small Day Cannot Hold: Collected Poems 1975-1980
Things That Keep and Do Not Change
Forcing the Narcissus
The Embalmer's Art: Poems New and Selected
Cocktails at the Mausoleum
Tarts and Muggers: Poems New and Selected
A Man to Marry, a Man to Bury
Becky Swan's Book
Selected Strawberries and Other Poems
Kiskatinaw Songs
The Impstone
Grave-Dirt and Selected Strawberries
Entrance of the Celebrant
Songs of the Sea-Witch

FICTION

Given
Cargo of Orchids
The Dancing Chicken
The Charcoal Burners

NONFICTION

A Taste of Haida Gwaii: Food Gathering and Feasting at the Edge of the World
You're In Canada Now: A Memoir of Sorts
Musgrave Landing: Musings on the Writing Life
Great Musgrave

FOR CHILDREN

My Love Is For You
More Blueberries
Love You More
Kiss, Tickle, Cuddle, Hug
Dreams are More Real than Bathtubs
Kestrel and Leonardo
Hag Head
Gullband

Exculpatory Lilies

Susan Musgrave

McClelland & Stewart

Published simultaneously in the United States of America.

Library and Archives Canada Cataloguing in Publication data is available upon request.

ISBN: 978-0-7710-9900-7
ebook ISBN: 978-0-7710-9930-4

Book design by Talia Abramson and Dylan Browne
Cover images: (flower) aqua_marinka / iStock / Getty Images Plus / Getty Images; (texture) KHALIL MUSA / Unsplash
Typeset in Australis by M&S, Toronto
Printed in Canada

McClelland & Stewart,
a division of Penguin Random House Canada Limited,
a Penguin Random House Company
www.penguinrandomhouse.ca

2 3 4 5   26 25 24 23

Penguin
Random House
McCLELLAND & STEWART

Stephen Reid
March 13, 1950–June 12, 2018

Sophie Alexandra Musgrave Reid
January 4, 1989–September 8, 2021

For Charlotte

CONTENTS

Exculpatory Lilies

PART ONE

THE AIR OF ELSEWHERE

WATER,

Fog Point (vodka) was made with water harvested from San Francisco fog.
— Gregg Hurwitz, *Out of the Dark*

Sloshed on fog, that's how I'd like to go, drunk
on immortality like something from a poem
by Emily Dickinson, whose last words
were, *I must go in, the fog is rising*. Wouldn't I love
to whisper something so specific when I succumb,
then sip fog with Emily in the afterlife, the two of us
on a storm beach cold with rain and sea-fret
passing the bottle, kibitzing about inconsistent use
of capitalization and our leisurely flowering
of consciousness, the awful letting go.
Emily wrote, "Water, is taught by thirst."
and I've always wanted to know, not why
the thirst, but why the comma? I might ask her
if I can see my way clear: fog has a way
of spreading its winding-sheet, obliterating
our life's words, complaint of rock against wave,
wave against shore. Words that rain, cruel words,
or kind, like the last words spoken to Jesus by a thief.
Words that weigh, like beached whales who smother
themselves under the greasy freight of their bodies; how
quickly we utter our final words and fail
to recognize them as our own.

A BEAK FULL OF WATER

> A hummingbird . . . the one who put out a forest fire,
> one beak full of water at a time.
> —Terry Tempest Williams, *When Women Were Birds*

I saw a wilderness on fire, birds falling in flames:
where was the do-good hummingbird then,
a question you might ask. She may have had
other fires to fight, trailing the night behind her
like a black sheet in her beak, over the boreal forests
of Siberia, on to the Similkameen. When she dips
to fill her beak in the Atlantic, the sea tastes
of the history of grief, and flying back through centuries
her head feels heavier than a Russian doll's—
six skulls, each one smaller than the last, nesting
inside one another, crying *water, water*,
in a language older than words.

WITHOUT WATER

(i)
a dying man reaches for the font of holy water
only to find that it's dry
—Joanne O'Leary

I cup water in my hands and it disappears before
my fingers reach my lips—no surprise, no mysteries there.
You told me, even our unshed tears can be holy.
How beloved you were, and now, gone.

I went days without water after your body betrayed you,
to see if mine would live, then buried you in the family earth
wearing only the gold band you wore in every photograph
taken since we'd wed. You swore your life had never been
more than a long preparation for the leaving of it; how could I
have saved you, so. What is left now, that I honour you as dust?
Even if the font is dry, you said, *drink!*

(ii)

the glow of the rising moon was yellow like the colour of water would be
if wedding rings were washed in it and the gold soaked off.
—Charlie Smith, *Cheap Ticket to Heaven*

I wash my hands in the river when the moon is new; the old
gold of my wedding band like a lure, everything that breathes
is drawn to it. The way you were once drawn.

I wash my hands, but how can I wash my heart?
When you left I took the ring from my finger and hurled it
at the moon's reflection, one night when the wild dogs
were for once silent but the grieving moon—I could see
our wedding portrait in her face—howled. The river turned
gold as it flowed towards the sea. You touched me like waves,
like rain, like morning dew, like no one.

I have the yellow eyes of my ancestors; from them
I inherited the moment the leaves turn flaxen in autumn,
and the devotion I have to winter when I become
the amber colour of water, waiting for you to drink me.

Just say the word—*water.* Say it again so I'll know
how much I meant to you, once. Say it again. Say *water.*

THE WAY WATER SLEEPS

(iii)
ice is astonished by water
—Jane Hirshfield, *The Beauty: Poems*

Each time a breath leaves our body, someone dies. With a day's
breathing we inhale at least one molecule from the breath
of every person who has ever lived. When I read this, I knew
that would include you, the one I love; you enter me once a day,
and rest in me the way water sleeps in ice.

Now I dare not exhale, lest you leave. Don't die, you
begged me; memories are so hard to hold. Our life together ended
with a flat line across a screen, a blip, a respirator's hiss,
and a young nurse whispering *he passed* to the doctor who failed
to arrive on time.

He is dead, I wanted to weep. Is it so difficult to say: *He died.*
The light around your body paled, there was a washed translucence
in the air and then—the astonishment of your last breath
brushed my face.

FIRST SIGHT

Love before first sight, that's how it was
with you. And now, thirty years later,
I go down to the river, filled with an old
longing. The river might seem unmoved,
but its beauty goes deep, as mysterious
as first love. I whisper the word *love*
to the cold north wind, and the wind
bows its head, ruffles the water's surface.
In the patterns the wind makes across
the black depths, our names, joined.

WHATEVER GETS IN THE WAY

For Stephen

The wind's from the southeast today, the day
you take the ferry to Alliford Bay, the Air Canada
flight to Vancouver. The Kwuna trembles, water breaks
over her bow. Love what gets in the way, you say, we must
love every obstacle.

Our last night together we watched the final episode
of *Narcos*, Season 1. There's not much left of Don Pablo,
which, I worry, is why Season 2 has met with a delay.

Did Escobar have any idea his life was destined
to become a mini-series on Netflix? He killed
whatever got in his way. But he loved his daughter
who begged him to buy her a unicorn for her birthday.
He bought a horse, instead, stapled a cone to its head,
attached wings to its withers: the horse died of an infection.

Pablo earned 60 million dollars a day and buried it
about the countryside. He burned bundles of cash
to keep his family warm when they were on the lam;
I like that in a man. His brother, the accountant, spent
$2,500 a month on rubber bands to wrap the bundles in.

I paid for your one-way ticket to Vancouver. The only
other time I gave you money, you threw it to the wind.

After a while, everything becomes
like marriage: you accept things
as if they never happened. Remember
those nights spent on a stone bench
outside the Church of Our Holy Redeemer,
not breathing until one or the other of us
got up the gumption to regain consciousness?
We had drugs we lugged with us in a purloined
leather bag, the initials HRH stamped on it
in gold; her Majesty's own physician had set
the bag down to attempt resuscitation
on the station platform but no remedy could rescue
that bad union of ours, the night train rolled
through it. If only we could lie together again,
hear the drums from the Big House
and the hard rain on the roof and the sea lions
barking like sad dogs out on the bay. Death,
back then, was something still intangible,
like having sex with the wind. Back when
we believed love would last forever.
That the worst had already happened.

in bed with the black cat curled against
my spine, listening to the rain, the wind.
I didn't want to rise, dress, take a taxi
to another airport, my body refusing to switch
from Irish time no matter how often I face
myself in the mirror and say *wake up
you are not in Donegal, you are not
in Sligo, you are no longer in Connemara.*

All I wanted—but then the cat brought a rat in
from the drowning rain—all I needed at three a.m.
Pacific Standard Time but, as far as my body
was concerned, 11 a.m. in Ballydown. I plucked
the luckless rat from the cat's paws
and dropped it in the compost bucket
full of old tea and swollen leaves, a happier
death, it seemed to me, but the shocked
rat revived: doesn't everything only want to live?

All I wanted was to return to my bed and spend
the rest of the night dreaming, but woke instead
screaming at Stephen because he was high
on pharmaceuticals. The sadness I feel these days
is no ordinary sadness; all I want is to lie down
with the sound of the rain on the roof
of my skull, the black cat beside me purring
its murderous self to sleep. But when I think

of Stephen giving up and going back to prison
even the rain is no consolation. I haven't felt
this much desolation since I left Ireland two days ago,
my mother in the aisle seat next to me
offering Mento after Mento, as if feeding my sadness
something sweet might pacify the grief.

You want sweet? I used to drive the frozen 401
from Kitchener to Kingston to visit Stephen at Millhaven
penitentiary: how many times I rose from my bed at three a.m.,
dressed and drove through the dark because I loved him
and believed, back then, that love . . . I believed, back then . . .
I no longer know what I tried to believe. Now the black stone
of my heart is sinking under its own weight, worn out from living
in the wet collapse of the wound for so long even death
feels unreliable tonight, in the faithless rain and wind.

STARING AT THE WINDOW IN THE CONJUGAL
VISITS COTTAGE, WILLIAM HEAD PENITENTIARY
APRIL 2011

There has to be a flaw to perfect
the view, a smear
on the window at eye level
where a child has kissed
the reflection of her inquisitive lips.
If I looked beyond, I could escape
into the wide sky that cannot stop
wild clouds from flying, but I can't
see further than this: the O
of her perfect mouth, my own
pointless lamenting. When I walk
the dark road to meet you, a stone
lodges itself inside my shoe: why
don't I stop to shake that pebble free?
It's as if we need the reminder, each step
of the way: it feels comforting,
the pain we obey.

When you enter the room, the air
of elsewhere envelopes me. Even
in the dark I can find you. The heart knows
what it knows: I should have been kinder.
I tried to kill the part of love that wants to live
more ferociously, hungrily, trustingly,
more heartlessly than either one of us.
I can't remember the crimes we are guilty
of, but when I hear sirens in the street you say
they're playing our song. You're so slick you could
raid the refrigerator before the light comes on.

EXCULPATORY LILIES

Good Friday, the day they delivered
that sad bouquet, was the day our cat
ran out on the road and failed to look
both ways. I'd stashed the candy eggs
under the sink, in their pink raffia nests,
safe amongst the household poisons
where the kids had been warned not to go:
on Easter Sunday before first light
I stole outside to hide the loot: the family
of bunnies in gold foil, the high quality
chocolate you insisted on buying—
nothing's too good for my girls! The lilies,
smacking of humility, devotion, had been
for me—your way of saying *sorry, I can stop,
I will lose the needle and spoon today*
but I was finished, I was through, said *sorry*
had been your default setting since the day
we vowed *I do*. I think, now, I was cruel.

The cat darted out, hit the car, staggered back
as far as our front gate; for a second, I thought
she might have been stunned, nothing more,
though the dribble of blood at the corners of her
mouth was a small grief with a life of its own.
I buried her at the bottom of the garden
where I had tossed your exculpatory lilies.

And where I picture them still. *Each new day*
above ground is a hard miracle, you wrote;
I hung on every miraculous breath you took
as I stood outside your door at night, dying
to hear you breathe. In the end, it wasn't me

you turned to, but God: wasn't love meant to be
more pure than faith, more sacred and enduring?
These days I lean heavy into the wind
and the wind's blowing hard.

THE WEATHER

This week's forecast, the probability
of grief. What's left of our life together
decided not to live, and it was you
who tried to rescue us, dialled 911
but reached despair instead. "If you'd like
to report a fatality, continue to hold. If you
believe in happily-ever-after, hang up
and try your call again." Driving through

horizontal rain to get home to you last night
I should have swerved when the wind gave me
the opportunity on that straight stretch
of road; I felt the urge. I want to die
needlessly, not after a long courageous
battle with *what-the-fuck*, not lovingly
surrounded by *who-the-fuck* giving me
a thumbs up for sticking around
as stubbornly as I did. I feel

the weather on us tonight, old darling, the sky
so black you'd think it was the only colour God loved.

It took you ten years to tell me,
I don't like parsley. Next came dill,
five years later. *Does this have lemon
in it?* you asked, only last autumn, poking
unhappily at a marinating breast. We have
had a long life together, my love. I knew
from the start you never liked anything
over-easy: when it came to marriage
we had reached an accommodation. Now
it's death I can't fathom.

We duck under the crime scene tape
to enter the hotel. Poets always stay
at the best places. A body is being
wheeled out on a gurney: another
day, another overdose. The next morning
the same, as I compose my shopping list:
cardamom bitters
fig bread
a mild sheep's cheese.
I think about how we become our illnesses
after a lifetime of trying to overcome them,
how soon there is nothing left, your life's work.

A SPIRIT IN HUMAN FORM

Even while you still lived it seemed
you breathed something headier
than air. Part gangster—you swore
no one would show up at your funeral
for fear of being made—part
family man, you were good
at what you did as long as you stayed
clean. Drugs don't care who they kill.
The lasting mark you left on our lives
was a bloodstain—albeit heart-shaped
because that was your way—but still
a stain. Grief's a whirlpool of possibilities,
all of them calling for change.

PART TWO

THE GOODNESS OF THIS WORLD

THE GOODNESS OF THIS WORLD

ONE

> Little children, little sorrows; big children, great sorrows.
> —Danish Proverb

(i)
Rely on the cave and one day
the cave will be empty. I find
no solace in being alive
though spring has arrived
and an east wind tells me
I should mouth a rosary
of gratitude: to what end?

(ii)
Break what is already broken.
Choose one form of emptiness
over another. Take this casket
of black earth and sit with it
by the river. Sitting is familiar
practice. Scraping dirt
from the bones of a daughter
is not.

(iii)
Find a word that tastes
of holiness. Hold it under
your tongue. Say it as you kneel
on the rain-wet street, begging
the north wind to blow
back the way it came.

(iv)
Don't ask why the addiction,
my friend says, ask why
the pain? I'd fall on my knees,
shout to heaven every prayer I've ever
faltered over to have you here with me
now. What can death promise you
that I never did?

(v)
Douse the fire before it spreads
through the black spruce
to the river's edge. Don't tell me
life is full of surprises: an arrow
is not just an arrow anymore
when it's singing into your heart.

(vi)
Remind me why I have spent
twenty-three years loving you.
Tell me grief has an end.
Tell me you'll grow out of it,
that we are not attached
to the outcome of this life.

(vii)
Ride an ill-fated horse
along the dunes; such a horse will
continually stumble. She'll get up
and fall, over and over again
as if trying to tell you: whatever
you think you need most, you'll find
someone doing without.

(viii)
Won't you find a way, always, of being
faithful to your demons? Death might look
like a one-way street to most people
but you, you figure you can sneak back up it
while the traffic is light.

(ix)
Stealing and lies, that's all
I remember of your dope-sick ways.
But when I hear *crack whore* I think
what must it feel like to wake up
at the end of your life each day, then walk out
into the world, empty-handed.

(x)
Rain follows you into the city,
strong gusts of wind flinging
dead leaves out of the sky. The year
is almost done. There is nothing
lonelier on God's earth
than a heroin addict.

(xi)
A good rider falls,
a good swimmer drowns.
A tired mother lets her long hair
down, as faithful as sorrow
on the burying ground.

(xii)
Praise the needle, the bent
spoon. The burned mattress,
the missing shoe. Your clothes
that belonged to a dead girl
whose name you never knew.

TWO

"It would be hard to define chaos better than as a world where
children decide they don't want to live."—Edward Hoagland

(i)
Imagine you call to say you are back
in treatment; you ride horses every day.
You've rediscovered dancing. Imagine you don't call
asking for sixty dollars. To say everything you own
has been stolen by a girl you thought you trusted.
Your wallet's gone, all that new ID. Imagine
if I did not have to lie awake thinking
how will they identify your body?

(ii)
Mourning you is what I do
best. But this morning I woke
to new snow, and a message from you
on Facebook: *I love you so much*
mumma. ill call as soon as I can.
You're alive. Snow obliterates
our house under a downy shroud.
But you're out there, living.

(iii)

Locked out, you broke in, smashed
a window so the orange kitten you found
in the dumpster could sleep in a warm bed,
watch cartoons on TV. You didn't want her
to feel cold and lonely, you told the cops
who arrested you in the morning.
How could I stop loving you?
You were always like a small bird
in an unexpected winter, your beauty
and mercy flying so high above us on this earth.

(iv)

My habit you called it, and wet the bed
each night, but so good-naturedly. I washed
and changed your sheets, scrubbed the mattress
with vinegar while you chattered about your dreams.
I've forgotten them, all except *I don't have any*
good dreams, mostly bad ones. Even then you were
damaged, like my bone china teacup with the hairline crack.
I was afraid it would shatter if I looked at it
too hard, but I never saw how perfect it was
till it was on its way to the ground.

(v)

I don't know what drew me to your room
to give you a last goodnight kiss,
but you'd pulled the covers over your head
and a halo of white light surrounded you.

I drew the covers back: you'd smuggled
your lamp into bed with you because I'd insisted
we switch off your night light. You'd begged
me to leave every light in the house burning:
you had nothing to fear—"I'm here," I told you,
as if even darkness would know better
than to mess with your indefatigable mother.

The light had melted a hole in your comforter
and your pillow smoldered. The fire could have
consumed us both, my love, but you would have gone
on sleeping. I took away the lamp, and the remains
of your pillow, but didn't try to wake you.
You'd known grief. You'd earned your sleep.

THREE

GOD LOVES A DRUG DEALER
—graffiti

She forced you to cut your hair, hack it off
in front of those you counted as friends but failed
you in the end. Next time she'd make you
shave your eyebrows too, she said, and sent you
back onto the street with what was left of your dignity.

This girl sells the heroin you can't live
without. She said she would donate your hair
to a good cause, like cancer, and I thought
trust you to find a drug dealer with a social conscience.

I have learned not to ask why, but then I opened
the door and saw you standing small in your nakedness—
the kind of nakedness that can never again be clothed.
I cried and cradled your head, while you, wise
as ever, said, "Mum, it will grow back, it's only
hair." But your hurt goes deep.

You were the child I suffered for, your long hair
streaming as you ran wild into the wind
with your imaginary friends. While other mothers
snipped price tags off back-to-school fashions
I sat by your bed in the Intensive Care Unit
watching your vital signs blip across a screen.
You were barely fourteen; you'd had enough

of being alive. I lifted your head from the pillow—
the summer sun had streaked your hair
faintly gold—and brushed thin strands from your face.
I could almost feel you want to live again, by the grace,
as your hair slipped through my hands.

FOUR

PERSONAL EFFECTS

"the wrenching nature of personal effects when the person they
belong to has already lost so much . . ."
—Lynn Crosbie

(i)
I go through what I have left of you: a Glad bag
full of syringes, the scorched glass cylinder
—*you buy a rose in a tube at a gas station. Take the cork ends
off the tube and throw the rose out the window*—
you called a straight shooter, scraps of Brillo pads,
Chore Boy, your brand of choice, a piece of coat hanger
to pack the steel wool into the tube. Condoms, assorted
colours. A tourniquet. A bag of bottle caps called "cookers":
*you put the dope in it, cook it up and mix it around, then you
draw it into the rig and slam it.* How much
you taught me; how much I resented having to learn.

And your journal, the entry you wanted me to hear
when we met for coffee at Habit: Chapter One:
The Sober Years. I said, "Aren't you jumping the gun,
baby? You haven't even been to rehab yet."
You looked at me with those round eyes
that seemed to say *don't ever stop believing
in the goodness of this world,* and said, "Mum,
that was age zero to eight. Remember?"

I remember. The moment you were born, how you
popped out of me, two weeks late, like a tiny, shiny
lifesaver. The first time I gave you a bath, then
lifted you from the water and balanced you
in my hand, where you quivered like a soap bubble.
I wondered then how I would bear the weight of it,
to hold all that mattered in the palm of one hand.

(ii)
You brought home suitcases
full of other girls' clothes, lost girls
who had gone back out again—as you put it—
on the street, using. None of it mattered
to you, but after I lost you the last time, I didn't know
what to keep or what to give away. So hard to let go
of what death has touched.

I imagine another mother with a daughter
like you, in a far-flung city going through
the red suitcase full of everything you possess—
the summer dress I bought you at Bliss, the white
coat you said made you feel good about yourself,
the heels I teased you about, that "come-hither" look.

I am so like you. I don't want to feel
anything, either. So when you phone, cut off
from me in your own world, I pretend you have died,
that you are calling home from your new afterlife.
I'm happy for you as I close my eyes and watch you
vanish into a stranger's body. Sometimes
I even recognize myself, the suitcase in my hand.

(iii)

We were driving. The heroin you'd stashed
for the journey ran out around Nanoose Bay
where we pulled in at a Rest Area so you could do your last
fix in the privacy of the blue Porta-loo.

I got out of the car to wait and found, in the dead grass
at the edge of the parking lot, a suitcase full
of someone else's life: recipes, spices whose expiry date
had been and gone, a bottle of vanilla extract—the kind
I let you sniff when we used to bake cookies together. Lately
you had taken to drinking the supersized containers
I bought at Costco: you said it helped you sleep
when the drugs ran out. I'd begun hiding it, and the knives
I found in your bedroom under your pillow. I removed them
without saying anything, so terrified had I become of your fate.

In that parking lot I unpacked cutlery, saucepans with lids
missing, a single baby shoe. I worked loose the knot
on a bundle of unopened letters with footprints over them,
then stopped as you came flailing back to me
because someone had dumped a lifetime
of family photographs in the outhouse toilet pit
and up until that point, it was the saddest thing I knew.

We got in the car and drove, trying to imagine—
had she been kicked out of her house, or had she run
away? Maybe she'd chucked everything
before checking into the rehab facility on the hill, hoping
to start anew? I didn't want to go on, I wanted to turn back,

open the letters, find a clue, a name, an address to return
the things to, but you said it was useless and I could feel
the panic rising in you and I had little strength left at that time
and I was driving and you need both hands
to hold someone who is suffering and does not want to be held.

FIVE

"You must have chaos within you to give birth to a dancing star."
—Nietzsche

(i)

We used to joke—you liked to sniff the glue
that held our family together—but this much
is true: everything in our house had been broken
and mended, over and over again. I felt at home
in all the broken places, as if I could only find beauty
in hurt things, the antique floor lamps
with irreplaceable parts missing, and stands full
of wrecked umbrellas nestled together like crippled bats.
I couldn't throw anything out because it was chipped
or cracked, or even when it fell to pieces
in my hands. My fault was in trying to fix *you*,
who taught me, *all life on Earth is the dust of ruined stars.*
Words for your headstone, carved by a hard-bitten wind.
When the dust settles, we're left with dust.

(ii)
You say you promise them you'll do anything,
if that's what they want to hear, but mostly
under all that promising, you're not really there,
you're a kid again, diving deep to retrieve a coin
of any description. The wild boys let you keep
what you came up with; you were the best
because you could stay under the longest,
coming up for air only when you had to.
But water is harder the faster you hit it,
and there was no slowing you down.
I stand at the river's edge, looking up
at the bridge, and see you fall and sink
fall and sink over and over, though just
when I think I have lost you forever
you appear to float.

SHE TELLS ME SHE MUST MAKE HER OWN WAY IN THE WORLD

I picked her up at the Dairy Queen
on Douglas. She came late, flying
towards me in a thin dress and old
cardigan, the sleeves pulled down
to hide her shaky hands. I knew it was her
by the shape of her teetering body,
legs bare, feet still pigeon-toed,
like her mother's. How hard we had tried
to correct this trait before the habit became
unbreakable, putting her to sleep each night
in shoes with a bar between them to urge
her feet in the right direction. I opened
the car door and let her in, stroked her
matted hair that felt, for the first time, uncared for,
damaged. Her skin—I won't talk about her skin.
She wore sunglasses with one lens
smashed out, and wept as I held her:
I thought you wouldn't wait.

We drove, I don't remember where.
At a stoplight she showed me
the abscess on her thigh; the doctor
said she could have lost her leg
if she'd let the infection go.

She didn't want me to cry. She said she was staying
in a nice motel now, with her new friend, The Kid.
Her friend is particular, refusing to crash anywhere
if he thinks there's a bedbug in the vicinity.

She needed forty dollars. She didn't want to work
because seeing me had made her weak
and it's no good getting in a stranger's car
when you're sick; men think they can do anything
when the mascara's all over your face.

I gave her forty dollars and another twenty more
because—well, what's the use?—then
drove her to Tim Horton's on the Gorge
and let her go. She begged me not to cry
but how could I not, and then I couldn't
stop, I wept and my heart, a heavy mother, broke
the way a stone breaks. *More weight, more
weight.* I lugged myself home.

DETERMINATION

The night I found your ad on Craigslist
I had set a box of blueberries on the table
to pick out the bruised ones, those
that were past their prime. I took a break

and looked you up online. I'd suspected
you'd left the escort service where they'd
given you a room, free meals, a counsellor,
in case you needed one. I'd felt you were safe
in that place and you learned new skills,
how to fold sheets, especially the bottom-
fitted kind I'd always struggled with. *Who needs
Martha Stewart?* you'd said, the needle marks
on the back of your knees panicking me as you bent
to demonstrate how the corners of the sheets
tucked in. I could still see the baby girl in you—
you sucked your thumb when you were doing it
with a john, you told me later, one of your tricks.

After you hit bottom, after rehab, you prayed, kneeling
every night at the edge of your bed, hands clasped
so fiercely I swore your knuckles bled. I didn't ask
what you prayed for, only watched the sweet press
of your lips like red grapes swollen with the summer sun.

The ad had read *call me, I'm lots of fun*. Each night
as you prayed, I walked out into the dark, walked until
my fears declined; hard to calm the heart when it leaps
so high. You need to hear your own footsteps
in those moments, to trust you tread the ground.

THE SOUL IS A TINY THING

for Sophie

The day you were born the sun
thawed the tears on your father's
face. We needed you, a flirt
of grace, your breath on our lips
like one long kiss. We could have spent
a lifetime together in that kiss. Today

you are twenty-six. You send me
a photo of your white wolf hunting
rabbits in the snow. *Who says we can't live
forever, lol?* Everything we are
comes from the dying light of stars.

The day you are cremated, a girl modelling a black hoodie
like the one I've chosen for you to wear, lights up my Facebook page:
I survived because the fire inside me burned brighter than the fire
around me. I hear you laugh at the irony as they fire up the retort,
a laugh dragged through the ashes of a thousand cigarettes, tokes
of crack, my sweet dangerous reckless girl, what could I do
but weep, the way I did when you were four, butting out
a Popeye candy cigarette you scored from the boy next door
for showing him your vagina through the split cedar fence.
I told you, *next time, baby, hold out for a whole pack,* trying
to be brave, the way only a mother could. Now I carry you home
in a plain cedar urn, the remains of all you once were reduced
to this smaller, portable size. Not even you would survive
the fire this time, your light in ashes now, formless as the divine.

PART THREE

GIVING THE WOUND AIR

is the moment before you are born, the moment
you hesitate to reconsider before your head
crowns. I know. And your second thought
might have been, *isn't it enough that the arrow
fit into the wound it makes*? but by then
it was far too late. Years later, when I had come
to believe loneliness is what I had been born to,
I watched a master of Zen archery fit an arrow
to his bow. He'd set up his target at the edge
of a cliff, where he took careful aim. The arrow
sailed high over the target, and plunged
into the sea. The teacher looked at me,
his inquisitive student, and shouted
                                        bullseye!
all I would ever need to know.

GREED

The first memory is pain. They slap you when
you are born, in case you forget to breathe, but
you cry instead—it's the first time you've been hit.
Crying becomes your first language; your first words,
I want. You say the words to yourself, never speak
them aloud for fear of the fist. Your father ends
each conversation with *don't talk back:* you want
more of everything—breath, laughter, words,
even more of your father. You've since learned
all you've got coming is the moment, but what
is a moment anyway, but a unit of time made entirely
of its own vanishing? *You'll be sorry*, your father
told you, the first time you dared contradict. You
talked back, said, *look who's talking.*

GIVING THE WOUND AIR

My mother called it infatuation,
a word I found infuriating when used
to describe the desperate love I felt
for my brown-eyed boy in grade five.
That my commitment could be so reduced—
love is just lust dressed up for church
my mother would say: whatever lust was
I pictured it as a comical affliction.

My boy called me Pigeon-Toed Pete: that's
how much he cared. I'd caught polio
when I was two, and had always believed
my turned-in toes were a consequence.
I have since learned pigeon toes develop
in the womb—the cramped space persuaded
my toes to turn away from the world. As I grew
older I tripped and fell over and over again—
my mother swore she should have bought shares
in Band-Aids. Then the Band-Aids had to come off
so the wound could get air and heal: the awful
tearing sound, a hurt worse than the cut after the fall.

There were the other wounds, the ones air
couldn't reach. Nobody spoke about those.
They said I was tough, that nothing could break
or kill me, and they were right. I am
wholly committed to the iron lung
they call this life.

IN THE BEGINNING

I have heard the dark hearts
of the stones that beat once in a lifetime.
—William Pitt Root

Auden's advice: harden the heart
as the might lessens—a lesson I learned
in utero. A decade later I spent hours closeted
in my room, singing *you'll never break*
never break never break this heart of stone
and now can't remember the name of the boy
who broke me. How different it would have been
if I had known, back then, a broken heart
is an open heart: imagine the possibilities!
Now my eyes follow the mist that has come
all the way from the end of the world
to follow the river to the place it was born.
I see what tenderness is there in the beginning,
before our first breath, and after that the hardening—
no way back but to bend.

THE LONELINESS OF WHAT MAKES YOU UNIQUE
FROM OTHERS

My mother carried him over Christmas,
roasting a turkey, making bread sauce,
Brussels sprouts we all eschewed, the usual
—yams candied with brown sugar, baby
peas, and plum pudding for dessert
with enough rum in it to keep my father
happy. She felt, she said, when I was old enough
for her to confide in me, like a walking coffin.
Her doctor told her the baby had to "come to term."

How can the dead know when it is their time to be
delivered? My father drove to the hospital that night
and parked illegally (the detail my mother remembered
most, after not being allowed to hold her stillborn boy)
smack outside the main entrance doors under
the expectant sign, MATERNITY.

When my father said I was so useless
I couldn't boil an egg, maybe it wasn't true?
I was eleven, my mother in the hospital
having her thyroid gland removed and Dad
probably felt useless himself, blamed
his helplessness on me. Still, sixty-odd years
later, his words revisit me each time I try
to work up the strength for failure
yet again, and make another meal.

My mother came home from the hospital
with a slashed throat and a new sadness.
She rose every day before we did, packed
our lunches, cooked the rolled oats we
were forced to eat. Her one complaint—
my father refused to wash the saucepan
she cooked our porridge in, left it beside
the sink for her to scrub when she came
home—he didn't approve of her working
and this was his way of wearing the pants.

We seldom saw the scar on our mother's throat.
She hid it under a choker of imitation pearls
and didn't wear anything she would call
revealing. What *was* useless was trying
to convince her she was beautiful, despite
the scar, or because of the scar. Yes, I see
now what is true. Because of the scar.

HE RUNS OUR LIVES LIKE TRAINS

Once, the one time in my life I arrived home
late from school because I had taken the long way
back, along the tracks, I found my mother in bed,
grief stitching together her lips, in mourning
for the loss she had feared since the day
I was pushed from her tear-shaped womb.
My father, who'd never touched a broom
in the long history of their married life, had swept
the house clean and started on the garage.
In his mind I believe he was sweeping away
all traces of me, so that they might live.

Last thing at night or at first light when I wake
to the birds shrieking on the river, I hear
my father's voice over the *swish swish swish*
of the switch. *You were late. We thought*
we'd never see you again. Safe at home
in his world so broken and so whole
in the same moment, this was my life.

No offence, he says, *but you've never been known for it.*
We were at St. Peter's, the family plot, and I'd cracked
about Dad's grave facing the wrong way—*everybody else
faces East,* I said, *and Dad's facing West.* I was right, of course
but it upset my mother to think he'd been buried the wrong way
and I said *there's no* right *way to bury a body, Mum*; the minute
I said *body* I knew I had put my foot in it. I shouldn't have

mentioned the headstone, either, my father's sketchy epitaph,
WITHOUT CHANGE. *It makes him sound like a cheapskate,*
Mum says, now that I've drawn her attention to it, *and your father
well, you never went without.* Dad's family motto
was, still is, SANS CHANGER but he refused, in life,
to have French shoved down his throat and Mum
didn't want him to have to choke on it in death, either. I said fear
of oral sex led people to say things like they don't want
French shoved down their throats and—so hard to leave unsaid
the wrong thing at the tempting moment—remind her
of that last Thanksgiving together, how my vegetarian brother
decided to come out of the closet over the needlessly slaughtered
free-range turkey saying *will someone pass the gravy to a homosexual,*
and my mother passed the gravy boat to our father
at the head of the table instead. My mother's lover says, as if
I hadn't heard him the first time, *no offence but to put it bluntly
you've never been known for it.* And by that he meant tact.
The ability to tell someone to go to hell in such a way
they look forward to the trip. Not me. I tell him go to hell

in such a way that he regrets his decision to ever go on a trip
in the first place, but now that he's on a bad one
he's determined to keep going, and takes off hell-bent in Mum's
Volvo and she starts to weep that I have ruined her life
and in retrospect, I see it was not tactful to tell my mother's
gigolo to go to hell at my father's headstone raising ceremony, *dead
but for the formalities*, I eulogized, *with a bright future behind him.
Your father could be a tyrant when it suited him*, my mother says,
defensively, *but you always had a roof over your head.* Oh yes,

that sodding roof, my father saying *you live under my roof, you live
under my rules* so I moved out and moved in with a mad
English professor twenty years my senior. When the roof began
   to leak
I said I wasn't going to let a little thing like having to put a saucepan
in the middle of our bed to catch a few drips come between us,
   but when
I turned eighteen and our love turned legal, I left. I think of him now,
the reason my father bought bullets for his Luger, the one he kept
on the table beside his bed. Mum wonders if Dad feels impotent
   today,

alone in the cold and dark with no one to criticize or berate—
*for God's sake close the fridge door, turn out
the goddamned lights, what do you think I am, made of money?*
To lighten his darkness she has planted a white chrysanthemum—
he used to say he didn't see the point in squandering money
on cut blooms for people who could no longer appreciate them.
I walk Mum to my car and take the old road past Tzouhalem

to Cowichan Bay for tea. Not far from St. Peter's we pass another church with wreaths heaped on graves, in faded pinks and blues. *That must be the Catholic cemetery,* says my mother. *They are always more generous with the plastic flowers.*

MY MOTHER VISITS HER BELOVED IN IRELAND

I've never known the word *airport* to look so
lonely, all seven letters, each one an orphan,
as we head out of Dunsany for the road
to Dunshaughlin—*you turn left*, his wife said,
then you scatter. My mother has loved this man
for thirty years, though he will never know.
I can't find the road and neither of us can stop
weeping, me for my mother and she because
she believes she'll never see him again. I take
her old hand and she turns her head away, as if
feelings are something a person her age shouldn't
show. *Have you seen any signs,* she asks, as I turn
onto the M4 by accident, a soulless
motorway I exit from after paying a mighty toll.

Earlier, while she sat in the parlour talking politics
with the man she has loved since even before
my father died, I went outside and collected
horse chestnuts from his drive: how else to pass
the time? Every fall my father hid horse chestnuts
in our house—he believed they would banish
the spiders my mother was deathly afraid of.
(I thought he was mad, but now I do the same.)
My mother told me, before we flew to Ireland,
she wants to be buried with the pebble she "stole"
from her love's driveway twenty-five years ago—
it's all she asks. I wish I could find her a lovelier stone

but the crushed gravel under my feet today feels
too ordinary in a lifeless sort of way. My tears subside
somewhere around Swords, when Mum starts to fret
she has failed to fill in her Taxback forms
properly: *each one is different, they go out of their way
to make it hard.* I wonder at how quickly the mind,
like the road, is diverted, and why I never take warnings
such as ROAD CLOSED LOCAL TRAFFIC ONLY
literally. *Your father was the same way*, my mother says
when I have to turn around and take the detour
I should have taken in the first place, then stop
for petrol because, as Mum has reminded me
for the two weeks we've been on holiday,
"we're supposed to bring the car back full."
I still haven't seen any signs, she says, and then,
when I suggest we check the map, *I don't want
to go home.* The world isn't big enough for this
much sorrow: is there anywhere, I wonder,
we can call home? I tell her we will turn around
go back the way we came, buy a house in the village,
she'll see him every day. *I don't care where we go*,
she says, but I know she won't feel this way forever.

In the next town we come to I see it finally posted:
Airport 4, and the wind blows through the vowels
of the word I wish had never been born. Planes climb
into the wind-tossed clouds, the sound they make
filling me with the vast sky's emptiness. And suddenly
we've arrived. The signs point to TERMINAL 1,
CARGO, MORTUARY, WAY OUT. Jesus, I think.

The Irish. The words *airport* and *mortuary*
have more than five letters in common; who needs
the mortal reminder at this time? I find the hotel, check in,
help Mum upstairs, then cut myself trying to open
the screw-top bottle of Chilean wine while she fights
with the locked window to let in the fresh airport air.
Let's not let a bit of blood spoil the end of our holiday,
she says, and raises her glass: *Slàinte mhaith. Slán Abhaile.*
I bandage my wound, pour another drop. *Good health,*
safe journey. Soon Mum's humming a rebel tune.

TENDING SMALL FLOWERS IN SPRING

My mother, ninety this spring, is fed up
with the deer raiding her garden. It hurts
too much, she says, to try and scare them
away. It hurts to be alive, to have to move
your limbs, to bend down and pull the weeds.
She can no longer kneel and when she falls
she can't get up again. I have known my mother

longer than I've known anyone. She can still
get around well enough to leave
a vase of small flowers—the blue vase
we bought on our last trip to Ireland—
in the guest room when I come home
to stay. She picks last year's pearly everlastings,
what she calls deadery—so tough
even the deer have forsaken them—
that thrive for no reason in the riot of weeds.

IDEALISM

Aunt Miriam eschewed *isms,* wouldn't allow
them at Copyhold, the farm she and Uncle Giles
inherited, near Horseleas, the Manor house
where my grandfather had been raised
and was now owned by a barrister, newly rich
with a footman and a butler whose mentally
ill son worked for nothing, shovelling coal
for the fires; it gave him a sense of purpose,
the barrister said, a reason to carry on. If only
all their servants were the same, he commiserated,
in no need of wages, which made them a burden,
and so intrusive. In the garden where we sat
taking tea under the giant medlar, Aunt Miriam
told her own war stories of making a single onion last
the duration of the Blitz, and pronounced my beef
bourguignon with its foreign airs and surfeit
of alliums, successfully excessive. I learned
during my summer on the farm that a handful
of *isms* had been omitted from her list—
impressionism was allowed, as long as it applied
to the artistic movement, one where stillness
produced a sense of unrest—and she had
exempted any word that applied *ism* to a personal
name, so that Marxism didn't count, although
it was otherwise an ideal candidate. Alcoholism
was acceptable, not so much a belief system
as a condition, cured by stiff upper lips

and drink. I was an idealist, Aunt Miriam
maintained, one who, having decided
a climbing rose smelled headier than a lowly
spud, believed roses would make a tastier soup;
she said I would have to settle down sooner
rather than later, I couldn't expect to be carefree
forever. In those days I carried everything I owned
in a blue rucksack, including the unopened
letters from a Viscount who had renounced
the notion of material existence and fled
to his step-mother's castle in Cork—at one point
I'd thought he might have been some kind
of a solution. I left England for Spain; Aunt Miriam
died climbing from her claw-footed tub
when she was eighty-six; Uncle Giles heard
the crash as he finished the last of the fry-up
she had dished up for him before ascending
to her bath. *Idealism is a mansion containing*
many different rooms, some more elegantly furnished
than others, my Viscount wrote (I'd opened his letters
once a suitable time had passed) in poor
orthography; he included photography of the castle
he would cheerfully share with me, though failed
to disclose an address. In Spain I found a revolutionary
who said *it used to be 'give me liberty or give me death,'*
now it's, make me a slave, but pay me, which sounded
more romantic in Basque. He taught me to take
pleasure, not in ideas, but in small miracles,
like breath. Peeling wild onions to savour the sweet
layers within. A thin soup tasting of rain.

TO MY CRITICS

My grandfather, on reading my early
poetry, said *even Shakespeare had to write*
a lot of rubbish to begin with. My father asked,
will it last? As in, would I achieve immortality
the way Keats and Shelley had—me with my
romantic verses about smokestacks from factories
and cigarette butts languishing (sic) in tepid
cups of tea. Another minor reviewer, dead,
I daresay, from drink, dubbed my early scribblings
juvenile skirt liftings. Critics, I am here to tell you
I never rolled the way Willy rolled; I don't plan
on being immortal any time soon and furthermore,
I have *nothing* on under my skirt, nothing

to get excited about. Except that when I lift my skirt
empires rise. I lift it higher, empires crumble.

The cup that cheers but does not inebriate,
my grandmother would say, those afternoons
at three while we waited for the water to boil.
They sold her special blend—black, robust—
at a shop on 4th Avenue; after she died
they stocked it until the tea shop closed
and a coffee house opened in its place,
offering herbal infusions for those
with more tepid constitutions.

I can still picture Grannie, who came
from a long line of worriers: in the middle
of a good fret, she assured me, there was nothing
more comforting than a proper cup of tea. Milk
in first (it rendered the tannins insoluble), a dash
of milk which meant a mere splash and nothing
more extravagant. She taught me—it was
presumptuous to pour milk into somebody else's
cup, a slippery slope to murder and beyond.

Next came sugar, at least six heaping teaspoons,
the sugar-spoon engraved with her family crest,
a bloody dagger and *I Mak Sikker* (I Make Sure).
Even from her ebbing bed Grannie insisted
we put the kettle on. When you are in control
of nothing else in your life, you could still make
a cup of tea the way you liked it—strong

enough you wouldn't need faith to walk on it,
sweet enough to float a bullet.

My grandfather spoke Latin at the breakfast table
over his All-Bran and two stewed prunes, read
Paris Match in the loo, referred to his many
grandchildren as *little cannon fodder*. What else

do I remember of my childhood summers? Raspberry
canes, sweet peas the length of the garden fence,
the English oaks my grandfather had planted
from the acorns he brought with him when he emigrated
after the first world war. Learning to sew, painstakingly,
play tennis, desperately, at Jericho Beach, the air sauced
with heat, the fierce walk home uphill all the way
to Trimble and 13th. Shelling peas on the back porch,
the satisfying *ping* as each pea bounced
off the sides of the stainless steel bowl. The potatoes
my grandfather planted in the boulevard, the humbugs
he kept in a jar on the mantle above the rows of Penguin
Classics with their intelligent orange spines; how I desired,
beyond all reason, those unreachable sweets and how
my grandfather, possessed of the ability to read my mind,
offered me one every evening after supper.

African violets on the windowsill, the scent of rose
geraniums. The Rock Cakes my grandmother made
using bacon fat before it was considered unhealthy,
and tomato sandwiches on thin slices of the solid
white bread my grandfather baked every Saturday. Salt,

freshly ground pepper, a smear of butter, mayonnaise
we couldn't afford at home. We took tea on the juggernaut—
what my grandfather called the well-braced garden bench
he'd built himself, in the basement where the shelves
were lined with my grandmother's preserves—peaches,
like wedges of wet sunlight, bletted medlars and quince,
gibbous moons of pears. Everything my grandfather built
was "well-braced"—the measure of a good carpenter,
I observed.

In winter when I visited, I was awakened each day
by the sound of my grandfather shovelling coal in the basement
to feed the furnace, a sound I found comforting because
I could count on it. Wading through spring snow on the UBC
endowment lands in search of his sapling oaks, home
through the woods above 16th Avenue where he would stop,
ignoring my impatience, to whisper, *Hark at the bird!*

You cherish them, then they are gone. What more can be said.
My grandfather's dying words were *sunt lacrimae rerum*.
My grandmother's *what is going to become of me?*

PATIENCE

n. A minor form of despair, disguised as a virtue—Ambrose Bierce

At the Deep Cove Elementary School Christmas fair,
on a tour of my granddaughter's class, I find a poster
no doubt put there to provoke me—Virtues:
The Gifts of Character—a list of 52 positive
(subjective, at best) traits, each one a vague abstraction.
(Restraint is not included, but Patience, tryingly, is.) I go
in fear of abstractions and worry
for my granddaughter's future, that she won't grow up
being able to show not tell, but embrace, instead, dim
concepts like Enthusiasm, Excellence, and Service.
Lucca is five: how will Enthusiasm help her cope
when she finds her white cat in the ditch, a bib
of flies at its throat? How can she hope to achieve
Excellence by learning to sing "Jesus don't want me
for a sunbeam"*en francais?* When the slow neighbour
boy asks to kiss her new breasts to make them grow,
will she comprehend Service? And Patience,

give me a break. At Christmas, Patience is
sottish. Impatiently I wrap gifts, knowing they will be
unwrapped with the same enthusiasm. I bake
a gingerbread house; it feels good to be of service, explain
to Lucca who Jesus is, who he's thought to have been,
without once calling the crèche a negativity scene;
I keep it all in. Until the boy next door visits
with his new dog and half an hour later the gingerbread

house lies in ruin. We've spent hours decorating
and our showpiece has become a muddle of squashed
gummy bears, shards of peppermint sticks and crushed
licorice twists: I want to weep into my one ounce
of cottage cheese—there's restraint!—but tell her
she must be patient, he's a boy, and the dog hasn't been
to obedience school yet. Lucca pipes up, "*Patience.
That's one our character gifts. It's super super
hard. You really want to do it but you can't keep it in.*"

She throws her thin arms around my body, determined
to keep everything in. If she lets go she knows I will
shatter, like all those sweet pieces at our feet on the floor.

STONE BY STONE

Thread has to go where the needle goes.
Stitch by stitch, I teach my girls to sew.

Like trying to teach
patience to a legless man
determined to cross the river on stilts.

Stone by stone he picks his way, not knowing
the water is deep. That he does not have
to drink the whole river dry
to know how it tastes.

My granddaughter calls the tree that grows
through the heart of our house a *Douglas Fern
tree*. I've told her how a poet, Ernest Fern,
built the house around this tree, almost a century ago,
insulated the walls with newspapers, too soaked
in rat urine now for us to save, including one
from 1932, whose headline reads *Mad Trapper
of Rat River Killed in Dramatic Shootout*:
he'd been an outlaw most of his life, the way
you were before I brought you home. Ferns,
rats, and outside on the piece of earth we say,
with certainty, is land we own, wind through trees.

THE LESSON

We bushwhack to a clearing to build
our fort under a cedar tree with low hanging
branches—a bunker with no windows:
looking elsewhere, I tell them, can be
a distraction. We arm ourselves with sticks
I whittle from a fallen alder. They are not
old enough to use a real knife but understand
the lesson: I cut myself when I'm not paying

attention. Of course we must eat. The kiddos
have brought snacks—animal crackers and four
raisins. *Mum doesn't like us to have sugar,*
they both remind me. (I've been known to dole out
five raisins for dessert, the rebel in me, I guess.) We break
the heads off the animals with our teeth, then their legs.
I ration the raisins for the tough times ahead.

And water? Their mother stressed
they should drink plenty of fluids but I
hadn't reckoned on summer, the holocaust
sun, the creek receded into nothing. I tell
my girls, *somewhere north of here, it is still
snowing; in another world, spring rain falls
as if the world is being wept.* I see goodness

on their peaceful faces as I instruct them—
pick up your weapons, men, strap your knapsack

onto the back of your heart and when the fighting starts
don't forget to sing. When each of us is born
the wind enters us and sings us through
a lifetime of remembering. Right or wrong,
what does it matter? Those who care least will win.

PART FOUR

STILL THEY CALL IT MARRIAGE

Our first winter together we rented Pilgrim's cottage
near Ballyconneely in the west of Galway, the wind-
tormented days spent desperately burning
turf; one night I found a mouse in the cutlery drawer
feasting on crumbs, and carried him out to the turf shed
where I released him. Our ancient neighbour, Val, who
had not yet learned to trust light bulbs, had a great strength
for the weakness, whiskey tasting of smoke, rain,
and the rogue Atlantic sea. I tried to pick a fight with Seán
when he stumbled in late under our old neighbour's influence,
so relieved he was alive I wanted to kill him. Does it get more
romantic than that? He wouldn't fight back, picked up his book
and pretended to read. I freed the frayed copy
of *Under the Volcano* from his hands and hurled it
on the guttering fire where it refused to burn, growing thickly
black. I didn't know, then, our love was doomed
to last. Watching as the mouse ran back up the path I'd so
recently taken, through the open cottage door into the sacred
heart of Mrs. Pilgrim's kitchen, where he resumed his meal as if
to remind us interlopers *wild and alone is the way to live.*

My first husband, a sombre dipsomaniac,
felt crushed when I expected from him anything
as insipid as sobriety. The second, an unrepentant
bullion robber, said my breasts were too small;
then, after augmentation, argued they were so
large he could barely afford to support them.
My third partner, a solicitor, complained
my cream-based sauces rendered him
fatally unattractive to the barely-legal secretaries
in his firm. For years I dilly-dallied. I carried
the bones of my dead husbands on my back.
Finally, my last prospect, a personal trainer,
impregnates me with the buoyant feeling
that comes from dropping the weight
you have carried for so long, heavier, even,
than your own crucified body, tendons
tightening across your lungs causing
asphyxiation, eventually. The way to prolong
life, he proselytizes, is to lift your solid flesh
on the nails that have been driven between
the small bones of your forearms, increasing
your personal torment. Hard to imagine a more
excruciating passion. Still they call it marriage.

I AM THE ONE

On that wild spit of land where I am
filled with a sense of certainty that my life
is no more important, and no less than
a handful of sand, we found a sea-lion, shot
in the back of the head, and further on two more
dead, the price of pilfering salmon from a fisherman's net.
He severed their heads with his Husqvarna—it got
biblical on that spit, I was sickened by it, yet I am the one
who took your hand and placed it where I was wet, when the
   heads rolled.

A MOMENT OF SUFFERING ALLOWED TO BECOME EVERYTHING

is despair, is misery, call it
what you will. Who planted so much
bamboo that I can no longer see
the sun? My ancient Chinese neighbour,
I swear he is responsible. He told me
birds and flowers in the poetry of the masters
represent prostitution. My flowers are not
thriving in the shade of his bamboo
forest. And no bird sings.

I don't come here often, I am not looking for a bar
crush or dance floor make-out or even
an afternoon roll in the hay with the arms
dealer I met online, his wandering
hands. (Does anyone even say *a roll in the hay*
anymore, let alone *wandering hands*?) If
I wanted a man who was committed, I'd go back
to 1967, to the mental hospital where I met the sweet-
talking English prof who ditched his wife and kids to be
with me because I was fifteen and wore lollipop white
panties with red hearts all over them—and because
he dug my anti-war poetry. (Does anyone ever *dig* poetry
anymore?) This was before child abuse was invented,
and statutory rape was cool as long as he didn't
reconcile with his wife for the kids' sake, and you
slashed your wrists and burned your Ban the Bomb
T-shirt in true flower-child-style retaliation. Still, dating
was more innocent in those days, before cute-a-gory,
non-date dates (includes alcohol, playing eye contact chicken)
and textlationships where people have love affairs
without having met. *Hooking up* is now called
on a thing—you're dating each other, you're committed,
but it's not all over Facebook

yet. I hail from a time when a selfie was a photograph
you took *by* yourself, of someone *other* than yourself.
Someone you might commit to after they laughed their head off
each time you cut *off* their head in the photograph. Not even
a beheading is so personal anymore, not when it's trending
on Twitter: the day Raif Badawi was sentenced to 1000 lashes
I Googled *how many lashes can one person take?* and up
popped a link to Hard Candy 1000 Lashes
Fiber Mascara Primer and the Secret to Liz Taylor's lush lashes:
a genetic mutation. Maybe the most dangerous place on earth

is the one where you feel safe, where the sensation
of light streaking your face is like the tears of somebody else.
We commit—adultery, murder, suicide, this body to the ground,
this body to the deep. We read *7 Things You Can Do to Make Him
Commit*, all the while wondering Why Is He Afraid to be
Committed? We take Advice and Tips from the Experts on Sex
Positions, Find What Dog Breed Your Man is Most Like. I don't

come here often. My attention span is shorter than a finger's
in a flame and every time I go online I see heaps of available
people, each one claiming to be *a happy person who really enjoys
hanging out with friends, watching Netflix and just being me—*
and if that's you—seriously? I don't want to meet your gimp ass
for a Gestapochino at Saxby's, I have no desire
to be paired up or *cuffed* as pairing is called in the digital dating
age, and if a player takes my bait it's catch and release time, this
commitment-phobe is all gone Pete Tong, Swayzeing
into the fadeaway future. Leave me the fuck

alone, that's my motto. I've turned off my phone, don't
sext me like you used to. Acronyms used in Online Dating Profiles
do not include LDAA (Loves Drugs and Alcohol) so long-term
commitment is, at best, iffy. No serenity tapes or whale noises
needed on this voyage; I pop a pill to help me meditate, and go

unconscious where I can be, committed, wholly, to me.

If I had to be the underwear of somebody
famous I would choose Leonard Cohen
to wear me. I would want to be blue
because blue's a colour you can feel, and how
do you think I would feel being
intimately associated with Leonard
and his private . . . oh, this could so easily become
a confessional poem, which it was never meant
to be. I would want to be smalt, redder and deeper
than azurite blue, more like the dusky purple I tried
painting the bedroom one smouldering evening when the sun
was going down and my lover had left town and Leonard
was on the front lawn wearing nothing but me.

TAKE JOY

I took Joy home with me because I needed her,
a companion, a lodger to help pay the rent,
but then Joy, who had been crushed in her heart,
lay in the spare room for whole days, somewhere
between death and dying, possessed
by a Siamese cat who bled through the spare comforter,
doing his best to die, also. It was as if for Joy,
we were both condemned to live.

I tried, I really did, to make a place for her
in my frettish heart, and give her time to grow
and cherish her, but grew to loathe her instead
as she took over my house, room by room, until I had
nothing left. After Joy changed the locks I became
unable to take joy in anything—the Lord, old dogs,
good food: I especially lost interest in *The Joy of Cooking*.

It is, I've read, a comely fashion to be glad
and in that spirit I bought *Take Joy*; a wise book
I'd been told to read because it would help me
make peace with Joy, but I couldn't get past the title.
Joy was everywhere: in sex, in my ultra-concentrated
dishwashing detergent. Christmas was the worst;
I was unable to sing "Joy to the World" without seeing
unpaid electricity bills, the blocked toilet she expected me
to fix. And oh, what joy, those weekly trips to the food bank
I got to experience, vicariously—the rich dishing out

leftover Halloween treats for the wretched poor
to eat. Suck it up, I wanted to say, we share small
pieces of our hearts with others and the more we share
the less we have for ourselves. When the cat finally died
Joy enshrined him in a satin-lined box custom-made
by a transvestite carpenter she refused to pay; she buried
her pet in the vegetable patch, uprooting my heritage
tomatoes in a sacred pre-dawn ceremony. Months later
after I fled the house to get shut of her, and my landlord
sold the property and evicted her, I heard she'd dug up
the cat's body and relocated to Burlington, Ontario.

That was the night I needed poetry to console me,
so desperate had I become, recollecting Joy, and found
a falling apart copy of *Moods of Love* by "Canada's most
personal poet," Terry Rowe. The book was inscribed,
haltingly, *How can I forget the most BEAUTIFUL
experience of my lost life? Always, Mark.* I turned next
to the dedication page where the personal poet himself
had written, *As always, for Joy,* but there was no way now
I could remember who Mark was or how this book,
dedicated to Joy, had ended up in my possession.

THE TRUTH

The hitchhiker I picked up
a mile outside of Masset
claimed he'd been enlightened
by buttercups, so many
that to stare at them too hard
would have induced blindness. All day
he had meditated by the ditch
and the moment I'd pulled over
in my Jeep Cherokee he knew he'd been
blessed, he'd been waiting his whole life
for someone like me. It crossed my mind
to tell him—those were dandelions, not
buttercups, but—how pleased I am
with myself!—I refrained.

SMALL EYES

We argue over whether the moon
is full—tonight, last night, tomorrow?—
and I say ask the cat, she is out there
in the moonlight, small eyes
wet with dew, passing through
this life while we, inside the house, bicker
about how else to live.

HOW TO LOVE YOU

While reading *The Portable Poetry
Workshop* for advice on how to start
a poem, I dropped a raw sugar cube
in the middle of the milk foam heart
on the surface of my non-fat latte.
The heart disintegrated, instantly,
but I need to tell you the drink tasted
sweeter because of it, so sweet
it hurt going down, the tang of sin.
I don't know how to love you
anymore. Help me, help me begin.

WHAT A BLIND CHILD SEES

Lao Tzu says there is no greater sin
than desire. What then of the desire
to attain desirelessness?

The blind child sees whatever you or I
imagine he sees. That's the trouble:
no one knows what a blind child sees.

It would be reckless to hazard a guess
but I'm going to because I've known
the days: behold, desire!

PART FIVE

WHAT IS LIVING

WHAT WE DO

when the wind bites into our skin
when a loved one is unkind, when
a freshly slaughtered deer rises
from the dead and teeters down
the stairs onto the strangely ominous
road; what we do, at first, is to feel
lonely, the kind of loneliness a bird
feels when trapped inside a chimney
flue, not knowing which way to go.
For a long time we might sit and listen
to the desperate fluttering of wings
as they surrender to the choking dark.
We might boil water for tea, stroke the cat.
We don't always know what we will do.
The doe lifts her head and I see where
her blood has pooled and it quietens me.
I walk with her in the wind a little way.
The lover who was unkind watches
how everything unfolds—the cat,
the trapped bird, the wounded doe.
He sees that to love and be full of fear
at the same time is to journey through
the helplessness of each moment:
brief, mystifying, unholy, done.

TENDERNESS

Two kingfishers fly into plate glass
windows at opposite ends of my house
in the same moment: what
are the odds? I expect they had been flying
towards one another for thousands of miles,
across centuries, or at least from opposite
sides of the river. No matter: same outcome.
Two bodies committed to the ground,
the hard ground, no time for prayer.
Does anyone care that I sit here paralyzed
with tenderness? Don't think
for a moment anybody cares. Suffering
only comes in two kinds. Yours.
And mine.

There is a moment before the kingfisher dives,
the eagle swoops, the small green ducks disappear
like the breeze in the low-hanging cedar branches
over the river; there is a moment before I name
the kingfisher, the eagle, the ducks when I am not
the observer, I am the dart of light, rush of wings,
the trusting wind; I am grace: an end of living
in awe of things, a beginning of living with them.

The raptor, still on his branch
above the river, remembers. The slick
fish forgets. The soft rain remembers,
the hard wind forgets. The body flying
its white flag of surrender, remembers—
a broken heart is an open heart: fear
a black swan rising from the river's depths
forgets to remember the raptor still
on his branch above.

NOT ENOUGH

The smooth stone does not say
to the jagged ocean, you are
not enough; the kingfisher
to the shining, twisting fish
in his beak, you are not enough.
The knife does not say
to the cutting board, you are
not enough. Where does this
message come from, the one
the mind says to the rest
of the body, daily, as we struggle to live
on this earth: you are never enough.

TO CIRCLE THE UNSAYABLE

Almost a full moon and I
am lost in the woods at midnight,
trying to find my way home.
An owl crosses my path, alights
on a branch and we stare each other
down. When I move out of his
sight his eyes follow me
anyway. We play at this, me
separated from my spirit, he
enveloping my spirit in his wings.

The tarnished spoon, the blue teacup
with the chipped lip. This pen, the one
I love best, missing its gold nib. The rain
combing my hair. The sound the herons make
when I startle them on the river.

The salal, the cedar, spruce, hemlock,
the river that empties into the sea
and every year changes its course.

The birds that wait at the river mouth
for the cockles and rock scallops
the tide brings them to eat.

Two a.m. I lie awake in bed trying
to remember the best recipe
for apple pie. I have so many recipes
for apple pie; the sheer number keeps me
from sleeping, worrying because somewhere
in the emptiness of the uncontainable world
there is bound to be a better recipe
for apple pie, one I might never discover.

SPIRITUAL PRACTICE

Some days I am so preoccupied by trying to live
in the moment, I don't see what is going on
around me. I have always tried, like the time
in Grade Two when the class had lined up
at the Health Room for an eye exam and the nurse
asked me to cover my left eye and I pressed
so conscientiously that, when it came time
to cover my right eye, I couldn't read the chart.

Today I was similarly abstracted, holding
the intention of being at home in my body, fully
present, on a daily basis, when I looked out
the window and saw feathers floating by.
I went outside to where it had begun raining
feathery down, and found the source—an eagle
perched on a limb of a dying conifer, intent
upon dismembering the shorebird in his beak.
He didn't see me at first, his eyes the colour
of late sun falling on wild grasses, but when
he sensed my presence his eyes widened
as if he had been blind-sided, and I felt an instant
kinship, a new lightness of being, as if I had been
hollowed out and filled with weightless feathers.
I went back inside to resume my spiritual practice.
You won't find home when you're blowing away.

A legendary beauty who dies
an ugly old beggar: how often
have we heard it, the body
too small for what's going on
inside. Why not an ugly young beggar
who dies a legendary old beauty? I wish
my life were larger than it is.

EMPTY BENCHES IN SNOW

I pass by, high above the sea, not stopping
to discover the names of the dead
each cold bench commemorates. The snow
is what I like best about these
empty benches. It covers the old names
with the tenderness of an old mother
under a hard winter sky called remembering.

It went well. That's what the man who helped take
my friend's life said after my friend drank a last glass
of Chilean wine laced with a date rape drug
and then allowed his helper to place an Exit Bag
from a box marked Party Balloon Kits
on his head, and pump him full of helium. *It went
well.* That's what the man said to my friend's wife
who waited in the living room, in her dressing gown
dwelling deeply in her own thoughts and feelings.

Whose thoughts and feelings—apart from her own—
might she have dwelt upon? The man said the inflated
helium bag rose above my friend's head like a chef's hat
before being pulled down over his face. I like to think
my friend drifted up and away into that unknown country
he had written about, but death that day
was the sound of one cold hand clapping as I made my way
back down my friend's driveway, which looked as if
it had been paved recently with crushed bones. *It went
well.* A person spends his life saying goodbye
to other people. How does he say goodbye to himself?

ON THE VERGE OF A NERVOUS BREAKDOWN IN CASHEL, THE WEST OF IRELAND

You don't die from grief. She said this
as she opened the gate to her sister Mary's
garden—Mary who died in a car wreck
the same day we received two flats of seedlings
she'd sent in the mail. Grief comes down
like a grave-digging rain, like the cries
of the dotty rooster in the potting shed
where two black kittens with starving eyes
make my world smaller, seem so much more
cruel. I weep each morning,
climbing the steep hill to Mary's garden
where the wind scatters the fuchsia blossoms
and gathers me as I walk. I button my coat
against the grieving day, then
as the wind blows through me anyway;
my heart changes, and in that
tender wavering, I let grief in.

RAIN

> The tears I shed yesterday have become rain.
> —Thich Nhat Hanh

I almost weep for myself,
for this, having to be human.
Did you ever hear of loneliness?
Did you? I let the days enter me.
I let loneliness be the choir
that requires I sing alto
when I wish to be a soprano.
I could reach the high
notes, I promise you, if only
I could learn to breathe.
I don't know how to breathe.
If I breathed I could be rain, I could
fall. How fiercely have you loved
your days? Have you? How few days
are left, what few hours. For now
I know this: *the broken bottles our lives are.*

THE WAY THE STUBBORN LAND GOES SOFT BEFORE THE SEA

That month before Kimiko died I saw her
on the beach; the foam, after a north wind
had blown all week, knee-deep.
These days when I walk to White Creek
I think of Kimiko, closer to death
than I was at the time, the way
she sat straight against a stranded log,
waiting. My father said, *look your last
on all things,* and I looked at Kimiko and back
at the sea, thinking this is what I will miss, too—
the surge upon the shore, the herds
of sandpipers jinking in and out as the waves
break and recede. Now each time I look,
I look my last, and then
I look again.

ELEGY

How many times I walked Darkstar to White Creek
and sat with her, happy, watching the gulls
headbutt the wind, the ravens dive into the knee-
deep foam. I'd feed Darkstar her last treat
and we'd head for home.

Tonight Darkstar is recollecting the life beyond.
What is it that separates the living from the gone?
She wags her tail. She drinks, she eats. It means
she's hanging on, though every mouthful of meat
has the taint of the slaughterhouse in it. The rain
doesn't help, the grief of it, nor will our tears
be enough to keep the cold from dancing
Darkstar outside to chase the wind; her going
saddens everything—the moon, the stars.
She who brought us light in darkness
has saddened away the sun.

The X-rays of my old cat show his heart
obscured by shadows. I ask, will he heal?
as the young vet hands me the vial of pain killers.

My cat no longer waits at the door—he has learned
the outside world is a place that can hurt him, what's left
of him—the small ache he has become in my arms.
I don't blame him. I don't trust the world much, either.

It is hard to know if he suffers much.
Who's in the wind. Who's left standing.

HUNGER

When I go to the river with my trouble,
and sit under the big trees, I see my girl again.

Her dress is the colour of soft butter.
Her hunger tastes of whiskey and rain.

Behind us is darkness, and darkness lies ahead.
The worst kind of pain is to miss someone
you've never known, and worse, never will.
The emptiest days are loveliest; only
people with desires can be fooled,
and I have none.

ACKNOWLEDGEMENTS

I wish to thank the many dedicated editors of literary magazines and the editors of anthologies who continue to publish the writers of this country, against all odds.

I am grateful to Their Graces, The Canada Council for the Arts and the British Columbia Arts Council for their continuing support, as well.

Many of these poems have appeared in the following magazines and newspapers: *Arc Poetry Magazine; Audeamus; Barehanded Poetry; Border Crossing; Fiddlehead; Freefall Magazine; Gutter* (Scotland*); The Malahat Review; Manoa: A Pacific Journal of International Writing; Riddle Fence; subTerrain; The Walrus.*

ANTHOLOGIES:

50+ Poems for Gordon Lightfoot (Old Brewery Bay Press)

Alive at the Centre Alive at the Center: Contemporary Poems from the Pacific Northwest (Ooligan Press; editors Susan Denning, Daniela Elza and Cody Walker)

Beyond Forgetting: A Tribute to Al Purdy (Harbour Publishing, 2018)

Desperately Seeking Susans (Oolichan Books, editor Sarah-Yi-Mei Tsiang)

Hologram for PK Page, for PK Page Trust Fund at the League of Canadian Poets

Noise Anthology

The Best Canadian Poetry in English, 2014; 2021

The Path to Kindness: Poems of Connection and Joy, (Storey Publishing in March, 2022. USA)

Worth More Standing (Caitlin Press, 2022)

ONLINE PUBLICATIONS:

Blowing Raspberries (Ireland); *Courtland Review; Dispatches from the Poetry Wars; Juniper.*

A number of these poems were published in The Reach Gallery Museum Catalogue (Abbotsford, B.C.): *Tales Untold.* The poems were written to accompany paintings by the artist Davida Kidd.

"The Goodness of This World" was the winner of *subTerrain Magazine's* Lush Triumphant Literary Awards Competition, 2012

Part of the same series, "Personal Affects," won second prize in the University of Victoria's 50th Anniversary Prize, November 2012—publication in *The Malahat Review.*

"Wild and Alone" won third prize in the Fish Poetry Prize (Ireland) judged by Billy Collins, April 2020 and has been published in the *Fish Anthology,* 2020.

First Prize for "Water,"—*Arc Poetry Magazine's* Award of Awesomeness, September 2020

"Water," was also published as a broadside by Arc Poetry, July 2021

"The Spinning Ever Want the Still to Spin" made the longlist—top 3% of submissions—Frontier Poetry Open, 2021

"The Colour of Water" (trilogy) was shortlisted for the Fish Poetry Prize, judged by Billy Collins, Ireland, 2021

A number of the poems in this book take their titles from words or images found in the daily meditations in *The Book of Awakening* by Mark Nepo.

I had always wanted to write a poem entitled "Exculpatory Lilies" ever since seeing the *New Yorker* cartoon, "It's been weeks since you brought me exculpatory lilies," by the artist Michael Crawford. When I finally wrote the poem, in May 2020, I knew it was time to "organize the storm," to bring these poems together under one roof.

© Dawna Mueller

"[Susan Musgrave's] artistic presence over the past forty years has helped create who we are. She is as important to us as Emily Carr."
—Patrick Lane, author and poet

SUSAN MUSGRAVE lives off Canada's West Coast, on Haida Gwaii, where she owns and manages Copper Beech House. She teaches in UBC's Optional Residency School of Creative Writing. She has published more than thirty books and been nominated or received awards in six categories—poetry, novels, non-fiction, food writing, editing, and books for children. The high point of her literary career was finding her name in the index of *Montreal's Irish Mafia.*